A Practical Guide to Teaching Reading Skills at All Levels

Jenny Ollerenshaw

A Practical Guide to Teaching Reading Skills at All Levels

Published by Advance Materials,

41 East Hatley, Sandy, Bedfordshire, SG19 3JA

First published 2003

© Advance Materials 2003

British Library Cataloguing-in-Publication Data

A catalogue record for this book is available from the British Library

All rights reserved. No part of this publication may be reproduced, stored in a retrieval system or transmitted, in any form or by any means, mechanical, electronic, or otherwise without the prior permission of the publisher.

The publisher has made every effort to trace copyright holders and obtain permission for copyright material. If any acknowledgement has been omitted, the publisher would be grateful for notification and corrections will be made as soon as possible.

Book and cover design by Glen Darby

Edited by Virginia Catmur

Illustrations by Sue Ollerenshaw

ISBN 0 9532440 6 7

Acknowledgements

The publisher wishes to thank the following sources for their kind permission to reproduce copyright material:

Page 17: Ça Science, les Vacances, Été 1999, ASSEM siège régional, Grasse

Page 18: © 2002, Peter Sahla & Barbara Weber, London, DuMont EXTRA, DuMont Reiseverlag, Köln

Page 22: 'Esquisse d'une philosophie de l'ADMD, Réflexions d'un adhérent', Association pour le droit de mourir dans la dignité, Paris.

Page 23: Ratgeber Gesundheit aktuell, www.gesundheit-aktuell.de, 11 November 2002

Extracts reproduced from Advance Materials publications:

Page 26: Facettes de la France Contemporaine: Lecture et Mise en Pratique, 2002, pages 71 and 72

Page 27: Aspekte deutscher Gegenwart: Texte und Übungen, 1999, page 46

Page 27: Aspectos del mundo hispano: Lectura y puesta en práctica, 2000, pages 11 and 13

Our grateful thanks to

Annette Duensing for providing the German examples

and to

Kathryn Aldridge-Morris and Manuel Frutos-Pérez
for providing the Spanish examples.

Contents

1 Why this book? — 6

2 Why is reading important for language learning? — 6

3 Students as independent readers — 7
    3.1 What characterises the independent reader? — 7
    3.2 Confidence — 8
    3.3 What latent abilities do students already possess that can help them? — 8

4 Types of reading — 13
    4.1 Pre-reading tasks — 13
    4.2 Skimming — 15
    4.3 Scanning — 16

5 Detailed reading — 20
    5.1 Words which are not key to the understanding of the text as a whole — 21
    5.2 Key words whose meaning can be guessed at or worked out — 21
    5.3 Key words which have to be looked up in the dictionary — 25

6 Supporting your students' reading — 25

7 Post-reading activities — 29

8 A final word — 29

Appendix: Useful morphological trends — 30

A Practical Guide to Teaching Reading Skills at All Levels

"He has only half learned the art of reading who has not added to it the even more refined accomplishments of skipping and skimming."

A. J. Balfour (1848-1930)

1 Why this book?

As language teachers we give our students plenty of reading exercises throughout their language learning careers, but how often do we take the time to teach them *how* to read?

We should:

- ☑ equip them with clear reading strategies that they can put into practice
- ☑ help them to reflect on the process of reading
- ☑ make them aware of the different types of reading required for different purposes
- ☑ encourage them to become actively engaged with the text while reading
- ☑ teach them how to use the text as a new source of new language learning
- ☑ give them the confidence that they can do it!

This book tells you how to do all of these things.

2 Why is reading important for language learning?

Encouraging our students to read texts in the target language is very important not only for preparing them for the reading components of their examinations, but also as a language learning tool in its own right. Exposure to both the written and spoken word is essential, and the advantage of regular reading is that students can work at their own pace. They can go back over the text as many times as they wish to scrutinise the language and structures. They can also see word and sentence boundaries that are more difficult to distinguish in listening activities, where words can tend to 'blur' into one another and where discourse features such as hesitations can interfere with the processing of a text.

Regular reading supports students' productive skills of writing and speaking. It also reinforces the learning of grammar and structures, as students see them used in a real communicative context. It encourages the acquisition of new vocabulary in context, develops vocabulary-building strategies, and increases cultural awareness. When students are well supported in their reading it can also serve as a great confidence-booster. They can get a real sense of achievement from understanding a text which at first sight appears complicated and daunting. Finally, it should not be forgotten that reading in the foreign language can be an enjoyable activity in its own right, particularly when students are able to seek out and read texts on subjects which interest them.

3 Students as independent readers

The ultimate aim of any teaching of reading strategies should be to help students become independent readers (i.e. readers who are able to tackle texts on their own without the support of a teacher, but with other support such as dictionaries) at a level appropriate to their stage of language learning. At the beginner and intermediate level this might only be to enable them to pick up a brochure, little leaflet or short text and to extract specific information from it. At a more advanced level your aim may be that students should be able to read quite an advanced article, to understand the gist of it, and to be able to proceed independently to a more detailed reading of it if desired.

Independent readers at an intermediate and advanced level are able to pursue their own areas of interest and undertake such topic-related work as may be necessary for their examinations. A tangible by-product of this reading is always an increase in both their active and passive vocabulary.

The important thing is that it is never too soon to start encouraging autonomy in your students. Students whose confidence and spirit of autonomy have grown through undertaking independent reading find that these spread to other skill areas, making them more confident and effective language learners in general. It produces students who are more willing to take the initiative and take more responsibility for their own learning. It also results in students who are more likely to 'have a go' in a real-life situation where they need to use the target language.

3.1 What characterises the independent reader?

The single quality that is most evident in successful independent readers is *confidence*. A great many students panic when presented with a long text, and many are frightened even by short notices that contain unfamiliar words. Students of average ability who are confident that they can tackle a text on their own will do far better than above-average students who are worried about their ability to do so. It is up to us as teachers to build their confidence so that they can approach reading tasks calmly, confident that they have the necessary strategies to cope without a teacher at their shoulder to help them every step of the way. We will be discussing more about how to do this throughout the book.

Effective independent readers are also reflective readers. They are conscious of what they are doing and how they are doing it. They are aware of the type of reading that is required for the task that they have been set in the classroom or examination, or have set themselves in real life, and have a wide variety of strategies at their disposal. Finally, they know how and *when* to use a dictionary.

3.2 Confidence

Students often panic when faced with what looks to them like a long and difficult text in the target language. As teachers we need to build their confidence and skills so that they can approach the set task set calmly, confident in the knowledge that they have the appropriate strategies at their disposal to deal with the text. If they are confident they are half way there before they have even begun. This confidence is the key to unlocking latent skills and abilities that they might not have been aware that they possessed.

3.3 What latent abilities do students already possess that can help them?

Many students approach the reading of a text with a mind like a blank slate. As teachers you will all have seen students submit the most ridiculous answers to questions in reading comprehensions, that, if they had stopped to think, they would have realised immediately were *highly* unlikely to be correct in the world as we know it. All human beings have a huge amount of knowledge about the world and how it works that they can bring to bear when reading. This background knowledge is arguably the most underestimated and underused resource that students possess. They can harness this knowledge to make intelligent guesses about the probable content of a passage, given the theme. It can also enable them to guess at the meaning of unknown words in context and to interpret synonyms correctly. Most students need to be told *explicitly* that they should be using this skill of predicting and hypothesising based on personal experience and background knowledge – they cannot be relied upon to do so automatically. We need to encourage them to read *actively*; reading is the interplay of what the students *bring* to the text and the *content* of that text.

Reading skills in practice 1

1 Pick a reading text appropriate to the level of your students.
   For example:

   ▶ An advert describing a house for sale
   ▶ A restaurant menu
   ▶ A holiday brochure
   ▶ An article on the dangers of irradiated foods
   ▶ An article discussing the pros and cons of animal testing for medical research

   Do not show the students the text – simply tell them what its theme is, and, if relevant, who the target audience is.

2   Then ask them to predict what the text will contain in the way of information and arguments. When they have done this, ask them to predict some of the vocabulary that is likely to occur in the text.

3   Next, ask them to give you examples of information, arguments and vocabulary that is *unlikely* to appear in the text. So, for instance, in a holiday brochure, you are unlikely to find:

   ▶ information on the relative costs of buying cars in different European countries
   ▶ pictures of the latest fashions
   ▶ addresses for local mental hospitals
   ▶ a discussion about national politics (unless you are travelling to a political hot-spot)
   ▶ information on job opportunities in the area etc.

If you prefer, you can do this exercise in English to show them that we are talking about reading *in general*, and not just reading in the foreign language.

The aim of the exercise is to show students that their own extensive knowledge of the world and how it usually works is enormously helpful, and in the majority of cases can help them to make judgements about likely interpretations of words or sentences in a text. This knowledge should not be underestimated, and students should be encouraged to make *conscious* use of it.

Reading skills in practice 2

Here are short texts in French, German and Spanish illustrating how you can help your students realise that they can apply their knowledge of the world to a reading situation:

FRENCH

STUDIO DE PIERCING A L'ETAGE
Aiguille à usage unique
Instruments stérilisés

NOMBRIL: 50 •   ARCADE: 50 •
LEVRE: 50 •   LANGUE: 65 •
SEIN: 60 •   NEZ: 25 •

Once the students have realised that the sign is advertising body piercing, they can make certain assumptions, based on their own knowledge. They can predict that the six things listed with prices against them are parts of the body that can be pierced. This prediction can be checked against at least one of the words (*nez*) that they probably know. Next, from their own experience, they can eliminate certain parts of the body as being unlikely to be on the list (although it might seem that nowadays all parts of the body are possible candidates!) – such as the eyelashes, the wrist, the palm of the hand, the finger, the neck etc. Although some of these *might* be possible in some circumstances, their common sense should tell them that a list of this length is likely to contain the more common parts of the body that are pierced. This will enable them to narrow down the field of possibilities. Such reasoning also helps students to disregard ridiculous interpretations. Therefore, in this instance, the word *arcade* is highly unlikely to mean *arcade* in English, as this is not a part of the body, and is an unlikely word to find in a sign advertising body piercing.

GERMAN

Vegetarischer Eintopf

4-5 EL Öl
oder
75g Butter
450 g Möhren
450 g Blumenkohl
300 g Sellerie
eine kl. Dose (400g) Tomaten
1 kg Kartoffeln

¼ - ½ l Brühe

Salz und Pfeffer
Petersilie oder
Oregano

Die Hälfte des Fettes in den Topf geben. Möhren und Sellerie schälen, waschen und in kleine Stücke schneiden. Blumenkohl säubern, mit heißem Wasser übergießen und in Viertel schneiden. Kartoffeln schälen, waschen und würfeln. Gemüse und Kartoffeln abwechselnd mit Salz in einen Topf schichten. Flüssigkeit hineingießen und das restliche Fett obenauf geben.

Auf 3 Stufe zum Kochen bringen und danach auf 1 Stufe 30–35 Minuten garen.

Den Eintopf mit Salz und Pfeffer abschmecken und mit gehackter Petersilie oder gehacktem Oregano servieren.

From the layout of the text the students are likely to guess that this is a recipe. By splitting the compound noun *Eintopf* they can then guess that it is a recipe for vegetarian stew. This enables them to narrow down considerably the possible ingredients and to reject the meaning of 'flower' for *Blume*. If they are not familiar with the word *Blumenkohl* hopefully they will be able to guess that it might mean *cauliflower* since it also contains the word *flower*, but at worst they should at least realise that it is most likely to be some kind of vegetable.

Brühe may well be an unfamiliar word, but the fact that the quantity is expressed in litres, coupled with the fact that it is a recipe for stew that so far has had no liquid added, should lead any student who has some knowledge of cooking to guess that it means *stock*. If they do not know the word *Petersilie* it is easy to guess that, coming at the end of the recipe with salt, pepper and oregano, it is a condiment of some sort, and is likely to be a herb, as it is an alternative to the oregano.

From their own experience of the world they can also predict what is unlikely to be found in a vegetarian stew, e.g. *Rindfleisch, Schweinefleisch* etc. (although some might have experienced that what is hailed as 'vegetarian' in Germany might well have bacon, ham or mince in it!). The method following the ingredients contains quite a few verbs that may be unfamiliar. Again, the students' knowledge of the world can help them make intelligent guesses about what they might mean. For example, *schälen* crops up twice, as the first step in preparing vegetables before washing and cutting them, and so it is reasonable to suppose that it might mean *to scrape* or *to peel*. *Würfeln* is a little trickier to guess accurately; however, knowing that the potatoes had been peeled and washed, the students would probably guess that they would be further prepared in some way that perhaps involved cutting.

SPANISH

CENTRO DE DEPILACIÓN
Personal cualificado
Técnicas laser y a la cera

- Media pierna: 50 •
- Pierna completa: 100 •
- Línea de bikini: 40 •
- Pelo facial: consultar precios

Students will probably be able to guess *bikini line* from *línea de bikini* and from there make the link with charging to have something done to your bikini line, to guessing that the sign is advertising a Hair Removal Centre. Some of the female students may be able to draw on their personal experience of using 'leg depilators' or 'depilatory creams' to interpret the sign more quickly, and then simply use the *bikini line* to confirm their guess. They may also be able to predict that *cera* is waxing by checking against the other technique that is listed: *laser*. Then, they can go on to predict other parts of the body that are listed along with *bikini line* and guess that *pierna* is *leg*, since common sense tells them this is the one part of the body that can be either completely or half waxed. They should also be able to reason that *precios* means *prices* not *precious*, since facial hair is highly unlikely to be regarded as such!

It is useful to go through the reasoning contained in these examples out loud so that students can see that a huge amount of deduction and intelligent guessing about a text can take place even before they make a concerted effort to understand the text to any depth. They should appreciate that this type of reasoning will not always guarantee an accurate interpretation, but is very likely to help them come up with a plausible one.

All students need to be aware that their own knowledge of the world might occasionally be inadequate for the task. Their imperfect knowledge of the culture of the target language community might sometimes make guessing more difficult.

Here are some examples of instances where the students might wonder if they have really made a plausible guess:

FRENCH

> PLAT DU JOUR
>
> Testicules
> de
> mouton panés
> • 10
> garnis Mesclun
> Prix net

GERMAN

> Abgabestellen für den Gelben Sack:
> Mülldeponie Heidestraße
> Bahnhof Süd
> neben der Fussgängerunterführung
> Den Gelben Sack erhalten Sie an allen
> Toto-Lotto Läden.

SPANISH

> TAPAS DEL DÍA
> Ensalada de palmito 4 •
> Manos de cerdo 4 •

4 Types of reading

For a student, the process of reading (from picking up a text to reaching a full or even partial understanding of it) is not a purely linear process. Many students are poor readers because they do not understand this essential point. They start at the first word of a text and try to read word for word to the end of it, looking up every word that they do not recognise in the dictionary as they go. They apply a single strategy (that of linear reading) to every type of text. This is an excruciatingly slow and unrewarding process that very often results in the student losing the overall sense of the passage.

It is vital that students realise that there are different ways of reading texts, and that different types of reading are required in different circumstances. Not all situations demand that students have a very detailed understanding of every aspect of a text. If they are in the classroom situation sometimes they may just be required to pick out certain key facts or figures from a text; sometimes they may just be required to understand the gist of what is being said. This latter skill is useful when they are working on their own reading documents for a specific purpose, as they will need to be able to decide at a quick reading which documents are worth reading in more detail, and which are not going to be worth pursuing further.

Students are likely to engage in the following three types of reading:

- skimming
- scanning
- detailed reading

As a teacher setting a reading task, you need to know what type(s) of reading you require of your students, and they in turn, need to be told what it is, or to work it out for themselves, if their reading is to be successful. We will discuss each of these types of reading in more detail below.

4.1 Pre-reading tasks

Before reading a single word of a text there are several things that students can do that will prepare them for the reading task, and focus their brains on what to expect. Many authentic texts contain non-verbal information that can help in decoding the text.

These include:

- typographical clues: different fonts and font sizes, bold print, underlining, italics
- the title, headings and sub-headings
- photographs and illustrations
- graphs, figures, charts etc.
- the way in which the text is structured in columns, paragraphs etc.

As native speakers and effective readers we subconsciously use all of this information when we read texts in our own language to make predictions about what the text is going to contain. In most cases of prose the title and subtitle (if there is one) give us a good idea of what the text is going to be about. Any accompanying photos, illustrations or graphs provide further support for predictions about the text content at this initial stage. It is common for the introduction to tell the reader what the text is going to be about, and for the conclusion to sum up and put the matter into perspective. In between, each paragraph often deals with a discrete idea or aspect of the subject under discussion. By consciously reflecting on this non-verbal information before beginning reading in the foreign language, students can begin their reading with a whole set of predictions about the content of the passage (and where they can expect to *find* certain aspects of that content) that in most cases will prove to be extremely useful. Earlier we talked about confidence being the key to successful reading. Helping students to develop their predicting strategies gives their confidence an enormous boost.

Here are some examples of texts where, without reading any of the main part of the text, students can glean a lot of information about its content simply from the main heading and subheadings:

GERMAN | **SPANISH**

4.2 Skimming

Skimming is the term used to describe reading for gist, in which the student skims through the text quickly, without stopping to look up words or battling over understanding particular passages. The aim is to concentrate on key words and ideas. It is a good idea to train students to skim through the whole of a text before trying to read it in any detail.

Before beginning to skim through a text, students should have performed the pre-reading tasks described in the previous section. They then simply let their eyes skim down the passage to determine:

▶ what the general gist of the text is

▶ what type of text it is (for example a newspaper article, an advertisement, a formal letter etc.)

▶ who the text was written for (the audience)

- what the author's intent was (to inform, to explain, to persuade, to describe, to instruct etc.)
- whether it meets their initial expectations/predictions

4.3 Scanning

Scanning is a very similar process to skimming, but when scanning a text students know what specific information they are looking for and aim to home in on this, while ignoring other superfluous details. In the classroom setting this might be because they have a list of specific questions in front of them, to which they have to find the answer. At a very basic level, they might be looking for something like a number, a date or a name. At the next level, they might be scanning the text to find some of the key words that are used in the question, in order to locate the piece of text that contains the answer. At a more complex level, they might be scanning the text to find vocabulary and concepts that relate to the question asked.

When scanning it is useful to remind students that headings and subheadings can help them to narrow down their search for the answer. When they think that they have found the section with the answer, then a more detailed reading of that section may be necessary to verify it.

A Practical Guide to Teaching Reading Skills at All Levels

Reading skills in practice 3

FRENCH

This extract comes from a brochure describing holiday activities for children. The task here for the student is to match the drawings to the correct paragraph. Much of the language is quite difficult; however, in order to do the task, the students need only scan the text intelligently. The key words (which in this case are almost all cognates) are underlined.

> ▶ **Robotique**: à l'aide de matériaux simples (bois, carton, moteur …), vous fabriquerez des robots futuristes, sortis tout droit de votre imagination. Un module électronique permettra la commande de ces machines à partir d'un ordinateur et d'un programme que vous concevrez.
>
> ▶ **Micro-fusée**: la micro-fusée est l'outil idéal pour s'initier aux techniques aérospatiales. A base de balsa et de carton, elle est propulsée par un micro-moteur et peut s'élever jusqu'à 250 mètres d'altitude, avant de redescendre au sol sous parachute.
>
> ▶ **Environnement**: si nous savons l'écouter, la nature se confiera. Si nous savons l'observer, elle nous étonnera. Pour la découvrir nous nous servirons de différents instruments dont les loupes binoculaires, des jumelles. Nous prélèverons des échantillons, nous analyserons l'eau d'une rivière, … C'est un véritable travail d'explorateur que nous vivrons ensemble!
>
> ▶ **Astronomie**: observer le ciel avec des jumelles, des lunettes, reconnaître des constellations, des planètes, mais aussi suivre notre étoile, le soleil.
>
> ▶ **Les activités sportives**: le canoë kayak, la randonnée aventure, le canyonning, et la spéléologie (selon le séjour ou le chantier). L'initiation à ces activités sera menée par des moniteurs diplômés.

Match the following drawings to the paragraph that they illustrate.

GERMAN

The following text describes day-trips for tourists visiting London. It seems at first sight rather long and complicated. The students' task is to fill the six gaps with the names of the sites described in the paragraphs. In order to fulfil this task they only have to scan the individual paragraphs for clues to the identity of the site. Their own knowledge of the world should be an additional help. The key words are underlined.

> Eton College, Oxford, Cambridge, Kew Gardens, Windsor, Hampton Court Palace

Ausflüge

_____

Sie ist neben Oxford eine der <u>ältesten und berühmtesten</u> <u>Uni-Städte</u> der Welt. Das erste <u>College</u> wurde 1284 gegründet. Die Kleinstadt mit ihren vielen Kirchen und Colleges ist ganz auf das <u>Universitätsleben</u> eingestellt. Einmalige Atmosphäre.

_____

Einer der bekanntesten <u>botanischen Gärten</u> Europas mit seltenen <u>Pflanzen</u> und <u>Bäumen</u>. An der Themse geleben, mit riesigen Rasenflächen, die man zum Picknick nutzen darf. Sehenswert sind die <u>Palmenhäuser</u> mit ihren gusseisernen viktorianischen Streben, die <u>chinesische Pagode</u> und der *sensory garden*.

_____

<u>Das Schloss der königlichen Familie</u> beherrscht diese idyllische <u>Residenzstadt</u>. Besonders sehenswert sind die Prunkräume und die St. George's Chapel aus dem 15. Jh....Auf der anderen Seite der <u>Themse</u> liegt das <u>berühmteste Internat</u> der Welt: _____

_____

Das <u>Schloss</u> wurde 1515-20 für Cardinal Wolsey erbaut und von Heinrich VIII. erweitert. Interessante astronomische Uhr, eindrucksvoller Bankettsaal, Tudor-Küche und Speisekammern. Wunderbare Gemälde alter Meister.

_____

Die zweite große britische <u>Uni-Stadt</u> liegt am Zusammenfluss von <u>Themse und Cherwell</u>. Sie blickt auf eine tausendjährige Geschichte zurück. Einen Besuch lohnt neben Kirchen und <u>Colleges</u> das <u>Ashmolean Museum.</u> Zu den Ausstellungsstücken des 1683 gegründeten Museums, eines der ältesten des Landes, zählen Schmuck, Porzellan, Münzen, Grabbeigaben und Skulpturen aus der Zeit der Pharaonen bis zum frühen 20. Jh. Die Stadt kann noch mit einem weiteren Superlativ aufwarten, einer der ältesten Büchereien der Welt, der <u>Bodleian Library</u>. Von überregionaler Bedeutung ist auch das Museum für Moderne Kunst. Sehr romantisch ist ein Sommernachmittag auf der <u>Themse</u> (hier Isis genannt). Das <u>Punting</u> sollten Sie unbedingt ausprobieren: Es geht darum, eines der langen Boote ohne Kiel mit Hilfe einer langen Stange vorwärts zu bewegen.

A Practical Guide to Teaching Reading Skills at All Levels

SPANISH

The following extract is an example of the type of texts found in science museum leaflets describing the different areas of the museum. The task is for students to match the drawings to the paragraphs that they illustrate. The key words are underlined.

▶ <u>Planetario</u>: Viajes estelares al alcance de todos. <u>Planetas</u>, estrellas, <u>galaxias</u>, todo el <u>universo</u>. La sala del planetario es el lugar ideal para grupos de alumnos, y la exposición puede adaptarse a las necesidades de cada grupo.

▶ <u>Planta de reciclaje</u>: Hoy en día se intenta reciclar gran parte de los <u>residuos</u> que producimos. En el área de reciclaje del museo se explican los diferentes <u>procesos</u> y se invita a los asistentes a participar activamente: ¡fabrica tu propio papel reciclado!

▶ <u>Robots</u>: De los más simples a los más avanzados, se presenta la tecnología de la <u>robótica</u> y sus fundamentos. Maneja tu propio <u>androide</u> desde el panel de mandos.

▶ <u>Experimentos</u>: La <u>química</u> y la <u>física</u> ya no son aburridas. En el pabellón de los experimentos todo es experimental: <u>electricidad</u>, <u>gravedad</u>, presión, etc. Todas las leyes <u>científicas</u> puestas en <u>práctica</u> para facilitar su aprendizaje.

Match the following drawings to the paragraph that they illustrate.

> With both skimming and scanning, students should remember that they are not actually required to read the whole text.

5 Detailed reading

In many cases skimming and scanning will not be enough – students will need to proceed to a detailed reading of the text. Here, again, it is important to stress that even if they need to understand the text in detail they will not necessarily have to understand every single word.

All of the pre-reading tasks listed in section 4.1 apply to detailed reading. When faced with a long article or text, we suggest the following approach:

▶ Look at any photos, illustrations, graphs etc., and read the title and any headings and subheadings.
At this stage, if there are any key words used in the title or headings that the students think are vital to the understanding of the text and that they cannot guess at, they should look them up in the dictionary.

▶ Make initial predictions about what the text might contain and/or brainstorm over what vocabulary might crop up.

▶ Skim through the whole text.

▶ Read the first and last paragraphs and the first sentence or two of each of the following paragraphs, in order to get a better idea of their content.
It is useful at this stage to look at the linking words that are used to connect paragraphs, as it will give the students an idea of how the text and any argumentation is structured.

Only when the students have been through these preliminary steps should they begin reading the text in a linear fashion. By the time they start doing this they should already have a good idea of the content of the passage, and the audience and purpose for which it was written. Having done the preliminary reading they are less likely to become 'bogged down' with the text.

As students become more advanced it is highly unlikely that they will read texts in which they know every single word. They will always come across unfamiliar words in new texts, and the truly independent reader is one who knows how to deal with them. As teachers we need to give students strategies to cope with these unknown words. These words fall into three categories:

1 Words which are not key to the understanding of the text as a whole, and therefore can be 'skipped over'

2 Key words whose meaning can be guessed at or worked out

3 Key words which have to be looked up in the dictionary

5.1 Words which are not key to the understanding of the text as a whole

There are some words that the students will not know, and do not *need* to know in order to understand the passage. They sometimes need to be told that this is perfectly acceptable. Indeed, they need to be encouraged to have confidence in their judgements about which words are not key to the understanding of the text as a whole, and can therefore be 'skipped over' or guessed at.

Reading skills in practice 4

Take a text and highlight some of the words that you know the students are unlikely to be familiar with. Choose both key words and non-key words. Then ask them to work out in pairs which words are key words and which are not. It is useful to talk through the choices as a whole-class activity so that students can see the difference. This task will be more meaningful if you choose a reading passage that has some comprehension questions attached to it, so that the students' reading and comprehension has a focus.

5.2 Key words whose meaning can be guessed at or worked out

Students often reach for the dictionary before trying to work out or guess at the meaning of a word in context. They should never use a dictionary as an excuse for not using their brains! All of the following strategies should be practised in the classroom and employed when students try to guess the meaning of a word:

▶ work out what class of word it is – a noun, verb, adjective etc. (Does it have an article? Does it agree with following or preceding word? Does it have an ending which indicates tense/number etc.? What follows or precedes it?)

▶ look at its relationship to other words in the sentence

▶ take into account the context in which the word occurs so that intelligent guesses can be made and improbable meanings eliminated

▶ determine whether the context in which the word occurs is positive or negative

▶ use word families – does the word resemble another word that they already know?

▶ see if the word has a cognate in English that makes sense in the context

▶ use any prefixes, suffixes and general morphological features (see appendix, page 30)

Reading skills in practice 5

Take a text and highlight roughly six words that you know the students are unlikely to be familiar with. Choose examples of both cognates and non-cognates. Ask the students to work in pairs or small groups to see if they can work out the meaning of the words, using the list above. Ask them to reason out loud in their groups. Once they have worked in their groups ask each group to report back on one or two of the words, giving their reasons for how they reached their decision. If their logic is faulty at any stage then other students or the teacher should intervene. It is important at this stage to give credit for logical thinking and intelligent guesswork even if the students do not manage to guess the *precise* meaning of the word.

Cognates – Cognates (words having a common derivation), also known as 'transparent words', abound in French, Spanish and German. English learners of these languages have the huge advantage of getting these words 'free of charge' if they make a slight effort. However, so often do we warn our students of *faux amis/falschen Freunden/falsos amigos* that we sometimes omit to draw their attention to the many cognates that exist in the language that they are learning and English. 'False friend phobia' on the part of teachers arises in the main from excruciating experience of students' productive work in which they invent words in the target language by slightly adapting the word in English. For this reason it is worth telling students that cognates are something to exploit in their receptive work (listening and reading), and to use with great caution in their productive work (speaking and writing), unless they are sure of their ground.

The following texts show just how many cognates there are once you start looking for them:

FRENCH

This quite complex little passage is from a leaflet produced by a pro-euthanasia organisation. Most of the cognates underlined are very obvious, and only a few are more difficult to work out.

ACCEPTATION DE LA MORT

La mort est le grand <u>scandale</u> de la <u>condition humaine</u>, <u>source</u> de <u>révolte</u> et d'<u>angoisse</u>.

Dans leur lutte pour <u>prolonger</u> la vie, les hommes ont remporté des <u>succès</u>. Mais l'homme est toujours <u>mortel</u>.

Un <u>adhérent</u> de l'ADMD (l'<u>Association</u> pour le Droit de Mourir dans la <u>Dignité</u>) <u>accepte</u> cette <u>réalité</u>. Après s'être battu pour <u>conserver</u> une vie <u>digne</u>, quand la lutte est devenue sans espoir, <u>maîtrisant</u> son <u>angoisse</u>, il veut regarder la mort en <u>face</u> et <u>choisir</u> son <u>heure</u>. Il <u>refuse</u> les lentes <u>agonies</u>, les <u>souffrances terminales</u>, la déchéance <u>physique</u> et <u>mentale</u>.

On <u>comprend difficilement</u> que cette <u>attitude</u> – la <u>dignité</u> de l'homme – rencontre une si grande <u>incompréhension</u>, une <u>opposition</u> souvent hargneuse, parofois mal<u>honnête</u>. Trop de <u>contemporains refusent</u> la mort et pensent lui échapper en <u>prolongeant</u> par tous les moyens une vie <u>dégradée</u> dont elle s'est déjà emparée.

In French students will quickly notice that the cognates tend to translate as the more highbrow words in English.

The following German text contains different types of cognates. Some are easily recognisable as they are still very similar to their English equivalent. However, others have taken on German morphology, stems or spelling, or else their development from the originally common word has been different. Here only those cognates that still show quite an obvious resemblance to their English equivalent have been highlighted. Words like *Tag, sehen* and *können* are also cognates, but are too different from the English words to be of obvious help to learners.

GERMAN

This text contains only one example *(boomen)* of the many anglicisms that have entered German in recent years. Students who are studying more than one language might also find that they might be able to use this knowledge to decipher some words. In this text, for example, a knowledge of French might help with understanding the word *grippal*.

Ratgeber Gesundheit aktuell

Erkältung in Sicht?

Drei Tage kommt sie, drei Tage bleibt sie und drei Tage geht sie: Gemeint ist die klassische, unkomplizierte Erkältung. Erste Zeichen sind Niesen, Schnupfen und Halsschmerzen, gefolgt von Kopf- und Gliederschmerzen, Abgeschlagenheit und Husten. In der Regel verschwinden diese Symptome nach acht bis zehn Tagen wieder, wobei sich der Husten häufig als die hartnäckigste Begleiterscheinung erweist.

Gerade im Herbst, wenn Nässe und Kälte den Übergang zwischen Sommer und Winter einläuten, boomen die ersten Erkältungskrankheiten, Schmuddelwetter und falsche Kleidung, sowie Viren und Bakterien von vielen erkälteten Menschen öffnen die Türen für grippale Infekte.

Therapie

Bis heute gibt es keine Möglichkeit, die Ursachen grippaler Infekte gezielt zu bekämpfen. Allerdings gibt es einige Mittel, welche die Symptome lindern und den Verlauf der Erkrankung erträglicher machen.

Erkältungs-Opfer müssen sich nicht unnötigen Qualen ausgesetzt sehen. Schließlich führen Apotheken breite Warenangebote von medikamentösen Gegenmaßnahmen –

wirksame Helfer, die die lästigen Symptome von Erkältungskrankheiten schnell und gezielt bekämpfen können: Beispielsweise gegen Halsschmerzen, „tropfende Nasen" und Hustenreiz.

Auch ist es wichtig, während der Erkrankung auf eine ausgewogene, vor allem vitaminreiche Kost zu achten. Vor allem bei Fieber und verschleimten Atemwegen gilt es, viel zu trinken; drei Liter täglich sollten es bei einem Erwachsenen idealerweise sein. Der durch Schwitzen verursachte Flüssigkeitsverlust wird somit ausgeglichen und der „angesammelte" Schleim umgehend verflüssigt. (…)

SPANISH

The following article on the economics of globalisation demonstrates the large number of cognates students are likely to come across in a difficult piece of this kind. As in French, the cognates underlined tend to correspond to the more highbrow words in English.

EL FANTASMA DE LA GLOBALIZACIÓN

Hay un viejo dicho económico que reza 'las economías grandes no crecen, se expanden'. Esta sencilla frase encierra la explicación del fenómeno de la globalización. En términos macroeconómicos es absolutamente cierto que el crecimiento no es algo tangible, sino la expansión, para que el crecimiento se haga así posible en términos microeconómicos. La globalización plantea muchos dilemas sociales y verdaderos quebraderos de relaciones públicas a las autoridades políticas, pero también representa un verdadero reto en términos económicos de cara a su ejercicio efectivo. No hay que confundir el concepto de globalización con el de generalización, pues los mayores errores de estrategia económica devienen de la falsa premisa de utilizar las mismas pautas de negocio en diferentes mercados. La globalización – en términos económicos – sólo será efectiva si se adapta a la medida de cada mercado, tomando en consideración todas las idiosincrasias regionales al respecto.

Reading skills in practice – 6

Choose a short text and ask the students to highlight all the cognates that they can find. This can be a real confidence-booster to students at all levels. This work can be followed up by a dictionary exercise in which the students search for other words belonging to the same word families. In this way they begin to become more aware of morphological patterns and trends, as well as improving their stock of vocabulary.

5.3 Key words which have to be looked up in the dictionary

Once students have identified those words which they cannot guess the meaning of, and which are key to their understanding of the text, it is perfectly legitimate to resort to the dictionary. It is very important, however, that they know how to identify correctly the word they are looking for (e.g. distinguish whether the word is being used as a noun or a verb) and select the correct meaning for the context in which it is used. Plenty of guided dictionary practice (as well as a good dictionary) is necessary for students to get to the point where they can work with a dictionary confidently and efficiently. When working on a long text, students should be encouraged to write down the meanings of words as they look them up, to avoid having to look the same word up more than once.

6 Supporting your students' reading

▶ Central to training your students to be good readers is giving them a sense of *confidence* in their own ability, and the knowledge that they have tried and tested strategies at their disposal. Encourage them to view reading like a detective or problem-solving game. They have various known and unknown elements and all sorts of clues, and their task is to put them all together to unravel the message.

▶ Before beginning any reading task make sure that the students have consciously thought about what type of reading is required of them. It is a good idea to make this a first step in any reading activity done in the classroom or set as homework, so that it becomes second nature to them.

▶ Give students time in the classroom to read in pairs or threes and discuss the strategies they use to decode the passage. Such conscious reflection and verbalisation can be enormously helpful and instructive.

▶ Set pre-reading exercises before students tackle a text. These may include any of the following:

  ▸ prediction of content and/or vocabulary (based on topic area, titles, subtitles, photos etc.)

  ▸ pre-reading quiz that checks how much the students already know about the topic (the same quiz can be completed again once the text has been worked on)

- skimming for gist and discussing initial impressions.

At this stage it does not matter if the 'answers' that the students come up with are right or wrong. What is important is that they are concentrating their minds on the topic.

▶ Make sure that you help them in every way to find the answer themselves, rather than giving it to them! Be prepared to give them extra support if necessary by using paraphrases, summaries, multiple choice etc.

FRENCH

Reading skills in practice – 7

The following example of the use of paraphrases is taken from comprehension work set on a text on unemployment and the 'Front National' in France. Students are asked to choose between three possible paraphrases for the given phrase. This exercise actually supports their reading as it helps them to work out the meaning of some quite difficult parts of the text. By trying out the possible meanings in the context they should be able to work out which is the correct one and thereby understand some of the more difficult passages or words in the text.

1 **le combat ... prend donc une nouvelle acuité**
   a) le combat devient plus intense
   b) on recherche de nouveaux adhérents pour le combat
   c) le combat devient de plus en plus difficile

2 **Les Français par naturalisation**
   a) les étrangers auxquels on a accordé la nationalité française
   b) les Français qui ont la double nationalité
   c) les Français qui sont nés à l'étranger

3 **...qui vise à faire des immigrés les boucs-émissaires de la crise**
   a) qui essaye de taxer les immigrés pour aider la France à sortir de la crise
   b) qui tente de faire que les plus touchés par la crise soient les immigrés
   c) qui essaye de faire des immigrés les responsables de la crise

4 **de nombreux immigrés ont participé à l'essor économique de notre pays**
   a) beaucoup d'immigrés ont contribué à la crise économique que subit la France
   b) les immigrés sont responsables de la crise économique en France

c) beaucoup d'immigrés ont joué un rôle dans l'expansion économique de la France

The following example is taken from some comprehension work set on a text about traffic safety. The students are asked to choose the correct ending to the sentence in each case. As in the French example, this can aid comprehension of more difficult passages by providing a simpler paraphrase of a difficult word or phrase.

GERMAN

1 **In den Städten soll es in Zukunft nach Ansicht der Grünen**
   a) viel mehr 30 km/h Zonen als 50 km/h Zonen geben.
   b) gleich viele 30 km/h Zonen wie 50 km/h Zonen geben.
   c) viel mehr 50 km/h als 30 km/h Zonen geben.

2 **Wenn ein Fahrer schneller als 30 km/h fährt**
   a) verbessert sich seine Wahrnehmung.
   b) hat er eine bessere Kontrolle über sein Fahrzeug.
   c) kann er weniger vom Verkehr sehen.

3 **Die Mehrzahl der verunglückten Kinder**
   a) waren zu Fuß oder mit dem Fahrrad unterwegs.
   b) waren im Auto unterwegs.
   c) spielten auf der Straße oder in der Nähe der Straße.

4 **Der dichte Verkehr auf den Straßen heute führt zu**
   a) einer Verminderung der Lärmbelästigung.
   b) einer erhöhten Luftverschmutzung.
   c) weniger Abgasen in der Luft.

SPANISH

The following examples are taken from a set of reading comprehension exercises on a text dealing with cultural stereotypes in Spain. The students are required first to match a series of key words from the text with their definitions. This is to encourage them to guess the meaning of the words from their context.

1 trayecto "durante aquellos largos trayectos"

2 variopinta "a la variopinta diversidad de origen"

3 tópico "lista de los tópicos nacionales"

4 desconfianza "mi íntima desconfianza"

a) Que ofrece diversidad de colores o de aspecto.

b) Espacio que se recorre o puede recorrerse de un punto a otro.

c) Recelo. Falta de confianza.

d) Estereotipo

Once the students have re-read the text in depth, some particularly difficult sentences are extracted and a two-stage translation exercise is provided to help them check their understanding.

> "Durante aquellos largos trayectos, con tortilla de patatas compartida y la bota de vino que pasaba de mano en mano, no había conversación que cuadrara mejor que aquella a la variopinta diversidad de origen de los sufridos viajeros."

Vocabulario:

tortilla de patatas: *potato omelette*
compartida: *shared*
cuadrara: *would fit*
sufridos: *long-suffering*

Explicación en español:.

_____
_____
_____
_____

Traducción en inglés:

_____
_____
_____
_____

7 Post-reading activities

Once the student has read the text and completed any exercises that were set, there is a tendency on the part of the student to set it aside thankfully, and never pick it up again. The student who wants to make genuine progress in language learning should plunder the text after reading it. (S)he should do some or all of the following:

- Trawl for useful vocabulary and phrases and make every attempt to use them in their own productive work.
- If this is not possible it is very useful to invent activities to use the new words by making up little scenarios or contexts in which it is appropriate to use them. Re-using or recycling the vocabulary actively soon after learning it from a reading text will help to 'fix' it in the student's memory
- Search for, note down and then attempt to re-use link words in the same way
- Analyse the structure of the passage
- Look at the register of the language used in the text and note down any interesting observations
- Take part in a discussion or debate that allows the student to re-use words, phrases and ideas from the text. Don't forget that vocabulary acquisition will be maximised if new words and phrases are used in different contexts.

8 A final word

Effective independent reading is a skill that needs to be acquired through active participation. If the students are to succeed, they need:

- Plenty of support at each stage to acquire the necessary skills
- Plenty of practice in class
- Good-quality feedback from the teacher at each stage of their reading
- Opportunities to work in pairs/groups to discuss the process of reading
- Constant reminders of what strategies to use
- Regular boosts to their confidence to remind them that they *can* do it!

Appendix: Useful morphological trends

Below you will find lists of useful morphological trends in French, German and Spanish. Students should constantly be reminded of these, as they are extremely useful in helping them decode unknown words. (Students should, however, be warned against using them indiscriminately in their written and spoken work.) A small amount of morphological knowledge can be a very powerful tool for learners, and boost their confidence enormously.

FRENCH

Examples from French

The adverbial ending *-ment* in French usually corresponds to *-ly* in English

1 Where the stem is easily recognisable as a cognate:

   exactement – *exactly*

   calmement – *calmly*

2 Where the stem is not a cognate, but should be recognisable as a feminine adjective:

   doucement – *gently*

   facilement – *easily*

The final *-é(e)* in French often corresponds to a final *-y* in English

   liberté – *liberty, freedom*

   armée – *army*

   probabilité – *probability*

   difficulté – *difficulty*

-ant in French often corresponds to *-ing* in English

   intéressant – *interesting*

   permettant – *permitting, allowing*

   appétissant – *appetising, tempting*

   parlant – *talking*

   prolongeant – *prolonging*

é- or *es-* in French sometimes corresponds to *s-* in English

    école – *school*

    études – *studies*

    éponge – *sponge*

    état – *state*

    épeler – *to spell*

    époux/-se – *spouse*

    espace – *space*

    Espagne – *Spain*

    esclave – *slave*

    espèce – *species*

Obviously some imagination and work is needed on the part of the student to recognise some of these words, but the relationship does exist.

ê/â/ô in French often corresponds to *es/as/os* in English

    forêt – *forest*

    tâche – *task*

    pâte – *pastry; paste*

    mât – *mast*

    châtier – *to chastise*

    hôte – *host*

This correspondence is not by any means universal, but it's always well worth a try!

Words ending in *-que* often end in *-c/-ck/-k/-cal* in English

    publique – *public*

    attaque – *attack*

    risque – *risk*

    physique – *physical*

GERMAN

Examples from German

-er (and *-ler/ner*) denote a person or thing that does something or carries out an action

> Computer – *computer*
>
> Rechner – *computer*
>
> Musiker – *musician*
>
> Sänger – *singer*
>
> Bäcker – *baker*
>
> Politiker – *politician*
>
> Redner – *speaker*

The above nouns are all masculine and usually a feminine version can be formed of those describing a person by adding *-in*:

> Musikerin
>
> Sängerin
>
> Bäckerin
>
> Politikerin
>
> Tischlerin
>
> Rednerin

The ending *-ismus* in German usually corresponds to *-ism* in English, and denotes a masculine word

> Vandalismus – *vandalism*
>
> Sozialismus – *socialism*
>
> Kommunismus – *communism*

Splitting long compound nouns up into their constituent parts often helps to make sense of them in context

> Tagesmutter – Tag + Mutter – 'mother during the day' = *childminder*
>
> Sonnenschirm – Sonne + Schirm – 'umbrella against the sun' = *parasol*
>
> Segelflieger – Segel + Flieger – 'sail + somebody who or something that flies' = *glider*
>
> Flugzeug – Flug + zeug – 'fly + thing' = *aeroplane*

k in German often corresponds to *c* in English

> Katze – *cat*
>
> Politik – *politics*
>
> Kaffee – *coffee*
>
> konservativ – *conservative*

sch in German usually corresponds to *sh* in English

> Schiff – *ship*
>
> Schaf – *sheep*
>
> schrill – *shrill*
>
> Busch – *bush*

Sometimes German words are similar to old-fashioned words in English

> Hund – *hound*
>
> Schwein – *swine*
>
> Mädchen – *maiden*
>
> Morgen – *morrow* (also as in *tomorrow*)
>
> schreiben – *scribe, encription*

SPANISH

Examples from Spanish

The adverbial ending *-mente* in Spanish usually corresponds to *-ly* in English

1. Where the stem is easily recognisable as a cognate:
   exactamente – *exactly*
   calmadamente – *calmly*

2. Where the stem is not a cognate, but should be recognisable as an adjective:
   dulcemente – *gently*
   fácilmente – *easily*

The final *-ad* in Spanish often corresponds to a final *-ty* in English
   libertad – *liberty, freedom*
   ciudad – *city*
   probabilidad – *probability*
   dificultad – *difficulty*

-ante in Spanish often corresponds to *-ing* in English
   interesante – *interesting*
   cambiante – *changing*
   relajante – *relaxing*

es- in Spanish sometimes corresponds to *s-* in English
   escuela – *school*
   estudios – *studies*
   esponja – *sponge*
   estado – *state*
   esposo/a – *spouse*
   espacio – *space*
   España – *Spain*
   esclavo – *slave*
   especie – *species*

Obviously, as with similar French examples, some imagination and work is needed on the part of the student to recognise some of these words, but the relationship does exist.

-ción in Spanish often corresponds to *-tion* in English

    acción – *action*

    educación – *education*

    emoción – *emotion*

-ico/-ica in Spanish often corresponds to *-ic* in English

    doméstico/a – *domestic*

    fantástico/a – *fantastic*

    económico/a – *economic*

-oso/-osa in Spanish often corresponds to *-ous* in English

    famoso/a – *famous*

    delicioso/a – *delicious*

    malicioso/a – *malicious*

Of course there are many exceptions, but it is a very useful general rule.

-ivo/-iva in Spanish often corresponds to *-ive* in English

    masivo/a – *massive*

    productivo/a – *productive*

    degenerativo/a – *degenerative*